About the author

Chellie Kew began her photography career in front of the lens as a professional model in the New York City fashion industry. Her work has appeared in a variety of well-known women's publications, including *Cosmopolitan*, *Mademoiselle*, *Seventeen*, *Co-Ed* and *Teen* magazines.

While living in South Africa in the 1990s, Kew found her passion behind the lens of the camera, capturing raw and upfront images of African children and wildlife in Botswana's Okavango Delta, Zimbabwe, Zambia and the South African bushveld.

Experienced in the operation of both manual and autofocus 35mm still cameras, Kew uses a personal technique to capture portrait, wildlife and photojournalism style images on high quality print films. Her photos have been purchased by individuals and corporations in the US, Europe, and Africa.

Today, her powerful images form the cornerstone of the courageous and inspiring story behind her mission to bring a brighter future to thousands of African children.

Her first book, *African Journal: A Child's Continent,* was published in 2003.

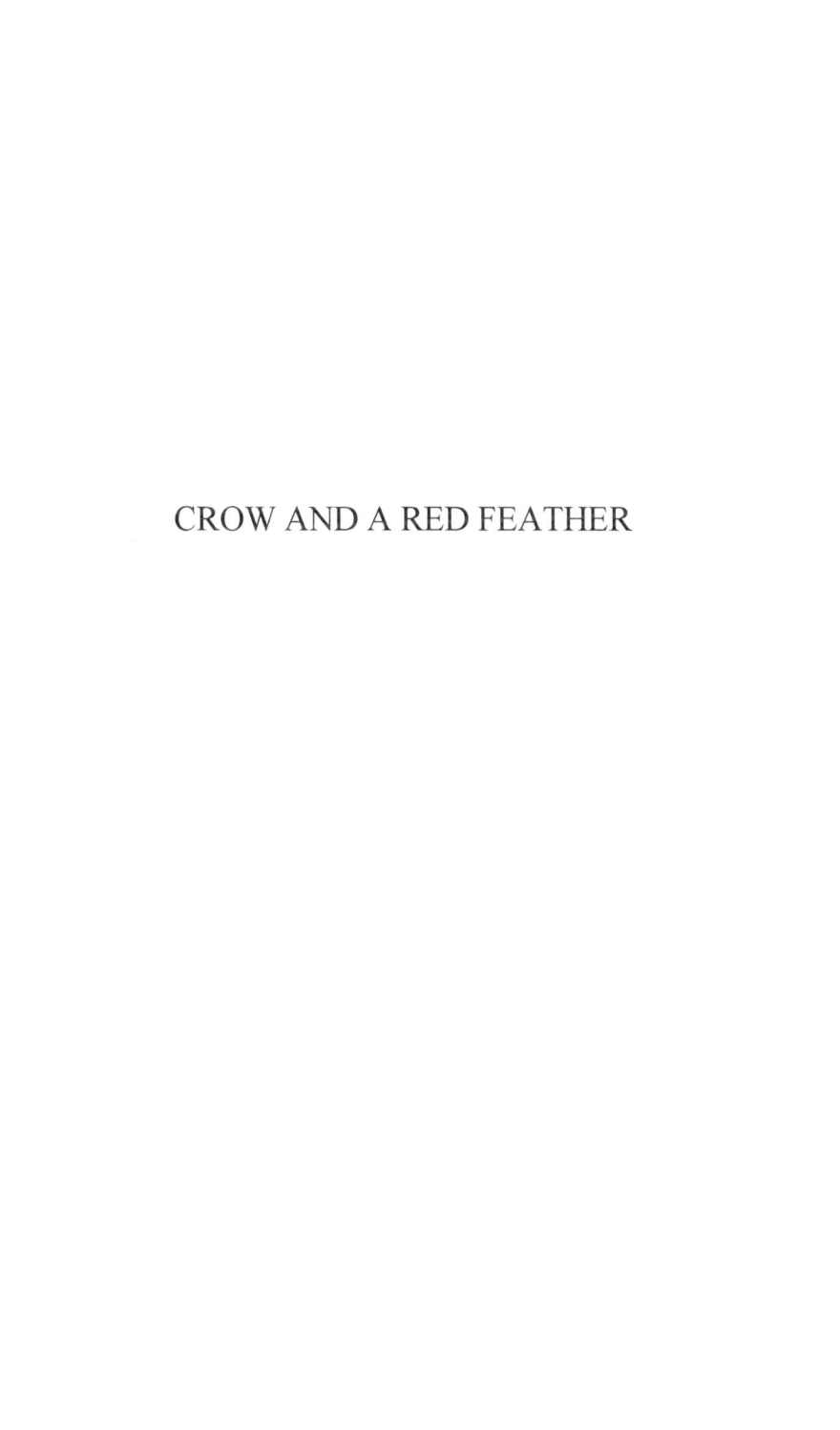

CROW AND A RED FEATHER

CHELLIE KEW

CROW AND A RED FEATHER

Vanguard Press

VANGUARD PAPERBACK

© Copyright 2021
Chellie Kew

The right of Chellie Kew to be identified as author of this work has been asserted by her in accordance with the Copyright, Designs and Patents Act 1988.

All Rights Reserved

No reproduction, copy or transmission of this publication may be made without written permission.
No paragraph of this publication may be reproduced, copied or transmitted save with the written permission of the publisher, or in accordance with the provisions of the Copyright Act 1956 (as amended).

Any person who commits any unauthorised act in relation to this publication may be liable to criminal prosecution and civil claims for damages.

A CIP catalogue record for this title is available from the British Library.

ISBN 978 1 80016 172 6

*Vanguard Press is an imprint of
Pegasus Elliot MacKenzie Publishers Ltd.*
www.pegasuspublishers.com

First Published in 2021

**Vanguard Press
Sheraton House Castle Park
Cambridge England**

Printed & Bound in Great Britain

Dedication

I dedicate this book to my mother Joan Blake, a playwright and poet, and one of three women to open the first all Canadian bookshop on Greene Avenue in Montreal many years ago. She held more faith in me as a writer than I had in myself. Urging me forward at every pass. Loving crow as much as I did. When given lemons in life, she made lemon drop martinis, danced and laughed, saying, "Things could always be worse."

Acknowledgements

This book would not have been written had it not been for the 'reading' told to me by Don Clarkson, a man who over the years had become a friend and trusted advisor, a gifted man who foretold I would write three books. Tragically he has recently left this world. I do, however, believe whenever a red-red robin comes around, it is he who reminds me that words have a price, to use them sparingly; that it is I who hold the red pen.

A huge thank you goes out to my dear friend, Alexandra terHorst. She not only believed that this book should be written, but always wanted more, as she corrected my dreadful punctuation. Alexandra and her husband, Pete, ran the PR firm that helped the 'Q' Fund grow.

I would be remiss if I did not say a sincere thank you to Vicky Gorry, production coordinator at Pegasus Elliot Mackenzie Publishers for all the many months of back and forth, over the pond emails, helping me bring *Crow* to fruition.

To my talented brother, Parker Wallman, who designed the book's cover.

And, to my daughter, Jeannette, my son, Octavio, and to my daughter-in-law, Mirta, who bring joy and meaning to my world.

Author's headshot is by Stephanie Ringleb.

Last but not least, all my dear friends who read this book prior to its completion, sending such loving comment, it brought me to my knees, weeping.

Chellie Kew, August 2020

Preface

My writing style, due to the dangerous and unpredictable areas of the world in which I worked, coupled with the assault against my body, mind and spirit, is that I write as if I were another person. I think of how the butterfly is first a cocoon, protected at the beginning only to grow wings and fly. Transforming into a newer, more beautiful phase of its life cycle.

The initial pen to paper buffets the realities of having broken my neck twice working boots-on-the-ground in Zambia and rolling the truck in Namibia. I can still today call up the feeling of sand meeting my bare feet—witnessing the space between the stars in the night sky.

During the writing of this book, I have lost too many loved ones. Forcing me to jump from state to state trying to find home. Trying to grab that tether that helps reel one in when the loss is too great. When all the while remembering the students attending a free community school built by the non-profit I founded years ago, educating vulnerable children. I reflect on how both students and their community have been made better by a group of caring individuals the world over. Maybe it's not a tether at all but a circle. The circle of life.

Crow

The crow is a reflective bird; all birds are. Eagles fly higher than any other winged creature. When sighted they signify higher thinking, truthfulness, the courage to look ahead to the rivers, roads and bends of life. A mockingbird mocks up to twenty-five different bird sounds. It can mimic a dog and a cat. Mourning doves, mate for life. Folklore suggests that red-tailed hawks move swiftly between the seen and the unseen worlds.

Birds sing a lovely tune to elicit a smile, or a frantic warning cry. Try as our feathered friends might that we humans rarely acknowledge the message. The birds' ability to fly upwards to a different vantage point to see anew — reframes and shatters old belief systems, or so the "two-legged" are summoned to take notice.

Melodies awaken memories to make us pause, to be watchful for life's signs, that we may change our beliefs, our outdated patterns of thinking. To disconnect what the mind holds as its most treasured calling card; regurgitated brilliance. Leap from that intrinsic, deeply rooted track. Stale and putrefied. A wagon pulled by a donkey, seeds once again sown, laid into the habitual row. Crows' songs invite us to feast on things above earth's realm. Soar as the bird. Offer up a new idea. A new perspective.

Namibia
March 13th to the 15th, 2002

Jet-black, a bird, indistinguishable against the backdrop of the African night sky. The absence of color: a time for ghosts, Ojijis and angels to play. Tricksters, or not. A paper-thin veil falls away, long before the coming sun crowns her head for a new day. Scattering nighttime's unseen to the four corners of eternity. Hidden behind earth's fold, atop stars and under the sea. They return.

Amber yellow eyes survey the damage of a white Toyota 4x4 overturned, stilled against the Namibian soil.

The black crow recalls this scene over and over many times during his lifetime. Out here in the desert wilderness one sees a lot. He cocks his head to the left, thinking to himself. *Fools to come and a fool to travel alone,* he screams in his high-pitched bird voice. His sunken ears, his entire head he uses to pick up any sound that may rise from the crumpled vehicle below. A truck, lit up by the constellations. Trillions of stars reaching down.

Heaven's staircases spin as whirling dervishes would attain enlightenment. He believes a woman is inside by the sound of her soft and gentle moan.

Ar! Ar! Ar! he cries. He pulls his wings in, bent by twin joints, shoulders, elbows and wrists, unfolding each, up and out in unison. Feet tucked in tight. He pushes out-stretched bones and feathers downward. Higher he glides.

The desert of Namibia is a haunting landscape. Towering canyons, massive clay sentinels stand, recognized as the castles that hover atop Sossusvlei. The name Sossusvlei, roughly described by Dutch settlers as 'dead-end marsh', or 'the land of no-return'. The world's highest sand dune looms more than one thousand feet above the orange flats that surround it. Like an endless reddish-brown piece of snagged material, a tablecloth laid out upon earth's floor, placed by the oldest custodians millions of years ago in an era long before Christ was born.

One might imagine with an aerial view downwards upon Sossusvlei, a massive sandcastle dragon quasi-set in a waterless moat; dried-out mud. Its elevated back-fin poised to whip its tail, as infrequent visitors walk along the highest ridge, disturbing disgruntled, contented laziness.

The harsh environment of the skeleton coast forces animals and plants to adapt to preserve water for survival. The shrub-bushes grow low to the ground. Small insects mutate to prevent loss of moisture from earth and sky. Hard rains arrive and exit on oceanic temperatures, as invisible hands pull an impervious screen across the Kalahari, leaving the ground drenched to scorched.

Namibia — the words parched, solitary, uninterrupted by space and time play out in the mind. The musical score, the notes that make up the keys, ebony and ivory, to the original melodies of mankind. Of life and loss. Hardship, struggle and joy. A song for birth, marriage, and a note for death.

The grumpy old dragon looks up at the crow; only his third eye moves, back and forth, a snake-like eye ever watchful under one laden lid. Crow tips in one direction and turns towards the other, both wings caught by the turbulent air of the brewing storm. Black on black, a band of white, iridescent. A checkerboard dot cartwheeling backwards against the pre-evening sky. Upset, he corrects himself. Crows are very vain. Crows are very smart. He rubs his wings together as a man would his hands. Crow savors sporting the mettle of bitterness.

While flying he searches, scans and surveys every element that surround this now distorted, picture-postcard landscape with piercing eyes. He remembers all things from yesterday and today, as he trusts he will the future. Or so crow would have every creature below him believe.

The night is still, but for a moment. Crow senses movement in the crash below. The smell of gasoline permeates the air, biting at the woman inside the now marginalized, standard issue African mode of transportation that has taken on the shape of an ancient beetle, the Egyptian amulet. The scarab was, and still is, worn to ward off evil, to give power to those that wear it.

She wakes but for a minute. Terror, hunger, thirst. Her first thoughts are for her children, her husband. She is injured. Pinned. The seatbelt jammed. She hasn't the strength to unbuckle it. How long has she been unconscious? It had been daylight, now it was dusk. It had been hot, now it was cold. She must hold at bay reality. Reality has come banging on the doors, wrapping its hideous face around the entire accident. With foul breath it steams the glass ruptured along the front of the up-ended vehicle, eager to make her his. "No!" she says aloud. *Focus on the bird's song.* Birds show up when she is lost. When she is scared. When she is sad.

In the distance the crow and she hear the violent seasonal thunder and lightning. Thunder, with its crackling crescendos, while its bedmate sets ablaze the sky in celebration.

Which way will it blow? thinks the bird.

Which way will it blow? This direction and in an instant, it will wash away the truck, thinks the woman.

We shall see, thinks the crow.

We shall see, thinks the woman.

Caw, caw, caw, he sings, as if to reassure, or to frighten her.

It is the near end of the rainy season. The crow opens wide his vision. Far up along the southern border of Angola the reddish sun slowly sets in the west; the landscape springs to life in silhouettes, as the unseen make the branches of the trees twirl as marionettes. Tall bushman grasses come into view. Grasses in colors of palest browns, softest yellows, pinkish lavender and blue green, while white rhododendrons and azaleas are in full bloom. Earth's rainbow dusts the floor.

Crow thinks to himself. He believes he knows what the outcome beneath his wings will be. Below, he turns his eyes to where the vehicle lays.

There is endless sand, a few squat-bushes. Boulders scattered here and there, as if placed by the stars above.

Crow still wonders what doom will unfold. What animal or man is near? His eyes' abilities are always filtered through a lifetime of grudges. Unforgiving is the nature of the crow. He says to himself; *She so far has done nothing for me to remember any maliciousness. Yet, I am certain I will find the need to attack her, or, possibly, save her. Squawk*!

Soul's journey

Shrills from above startle the woman. She tastes blood and gasoline at the back of her throat, licking the blood from her hands, and using her hands to wash her face. Futile attempts at safety, as both are tart scents to the predators, delicious treats. She is in leopard country: the leopard is everywhere in the Namibian dessert, like the street strays of Rome. The bugs make a hullabaloo. Malaria kills. She can feel her élan vital, her life-force, shedding its earthly tether. Her eyes become stellar as she drifts upwards alongside the bird. She sees all that lies below. All that is above.

The planets rotate. The galaxy infuses a kaleidoscope of refraction; light and sound, as an adult conch shell placed over one's ear, the gentle lull of the oceans ebb and flow. She is Antoine de Saint-Exupery's *Le Petit Prince*. The Little Prince.

High above the ground we hover; black and white. He and I, a murder of crows we equate. We look down on the scene. A truck halfway upside down. Front left wheel hooked up high on the right embankment. We comb the road ahead and behind to see the farm where she stopped to fill the empty tank of gasoline. Both stare down, at the skeleton coast, lit up, bolts of lightning licking the tips of some whitecaps. Dark angry waves come crashing to the shore, nipping at the long-ago forgotten sun-bleached fallen trees that now hold the framework of giant's bones.

Further north we travel. A small herd of elephants slowly makes its way to the watering hole. A parade, led by its matriarch, walk in the enlarged imprints of the elephants before. Pads on feet so thick their track is silent. Groups of animals have already congregated. Zebra, giraffe, hyena, impala, kudu and a pride of lions.

She and crow search to see if there are any fires on the ground below. The Himba light fires. The Himba people are one of the oldest living society of nomads who roam along the northern ridge of Namibia. They believe that when the smoke rises up to the heavens, a pathway opens up between ancestors and the living. A channel for communication. A conduit to remind them of the old ways of survival. Of respect, honor. Retold through the burn in the air. The sanctitude of all living creatures.

Traditionally small in numbers, the Himba, with their exquisite clay-colored skin, call the group 'family'. The women, their hair a mixture of ochre and mud, intricately styled starting from early childhood, layer upon layer of earth's rich, moist clay woven into strands, reminiscent of a tall honeycombed structure. An architectural merriment. Escaping dreadlocks cascade downward past a young girl's shoulders. Dressed scantily, both male and female tie a piece of tan fabric around their waist, baring sturdy coco-colored thighs. The mothers' soft breasts are exposed, making it easy to nurse a child while on the move. Their walk powerful, steadfast, a nobility of gait.

Ojiji

A far away noise pulls her back to the truck. Outside the truck looking in, she stands, her feet barely touching the cold, hard ground below. From somewhere, maybe a ghost, maybe her Ojiji; the shadow that follows its owner and awaits his or her return to heaven when he or she dies. A sudden flurry of wind whispers upwards along her spine. With each breath, she hears, *Push the truck, push it over. Push hard.*

On tiptoe, bending over the roof of the vehicle, she sees herself eerily cast in the glow of its interior overhead light. Limp, restrained by the seatbelt, her head slumped to the left. Blood masks her face. Her hands lay lifeless, her eyes are closed. She is wearing a white tee-shirt, navy cargo shorts. A red handkerchief is tied around her neck. Thick socks tucked inside well-worn hiking boots lay in disarray. Crow makes himself comfortable at her left, looking at her looking at herself from atop the exterior side mirror. Crow cocks his head to the right, then to the left as if in question. As if in judgment.

Her glasses are in the far rear of the truck. The bottles of water purchased are under the vehicle, alongside her crushed camera. All around her are broken fragments of shattered glass, tiny crystals that sparkle as diamonds. Her senses are heightened; the songs of the wind are heard, the buzz of the bugs. The birds make noises and the desert smells new — a rich scent, ripe and fertile — awakening under an unbuttoned dusty old overcoat. She chooses life. The earth has cooled down. Her vitality, her inner-essence accordions behind her as she slips back inside her human shell.

Unfasten the seatbelt, barefoot. Step up and over the stick shift. Glass gnaws the bottom of her feet. Find her cell phone, dial the three numbers for emergency. She is unprepared for the recording, a metallic English accent advising, "You are presently out of network range." She presses hard against the truck's horn. The sound is lost in the vast open space. Tick-tock, tick-tock, sounds the indicator, hit by mistake. Wrapping the maps around her shoulders for warmth, brings to mind the first time her bare foot touched African soil.

Johannesburg, South Africa
Fall, 1997

She arrives to a raw untamable land of unsurpassed beauty and suppressed beating rage. The pendulum swings far out to the left, and far out to the right, never resting at its center point, the place where calm is found. In Africa, she senses she will live in a world of seduction, felt as it rises from a geopathic force. A scorching energy claiming any and all whose internal compass is out of balance. She will view death, disease and dying, and in the same instance see joy, compassion and generosity. She will come to know Africa as her home, her roots. Its people as her people.

Up from the ground comes a vine, and on this vine is scored ancient knowledge; the souls' wisdom puts mortals' thoughts to shame. Around and around the green climber circles her foot, calf and torso, to continue its spiraling motion upwards towards the sky and beyond. She stands with arms open wide to embrace the cradle of mankind. She is reconnected to self. It matters not the color of her skin, for rushing through her veins is the remembrance of war, persecution and strife against a mighty and gentle people. She will come to understand it is the children of Africa who will capture her heart and call her back in her dreams.

Is the accident the premonition foretold by the psychic the night of the full moon? The night that began what was to become fifteen years of her life. In and out of Africa. Wasn't it her assignment to take photographs of vulnerable children? Was she not told to use the lens of her camera, zoom in on the beauty of each child, and not on their disease? Change the view of orphaned children living throughout Sub-Saharan Africa from one of death and dying to that of beauty and innocence. Find that glimmer of hope captured within the camera's aperture, a child's desire to survive. A child's need to be loved, wanted, held. To be cherished.

Leave other photographers free to snap images paid for by international publications to arouse emotion: The flies that cover eyes, bellies swollen. Parasites that render the second gut-brain, the entire digestive system, bloated and bilious. She senses that onlookers, visitors, fearful of contracting poverty, will turn their eyes inward, unable to focus on what is in plain sight. She has seen this indifference to human life before.

She remembers that the birds are the messengers from God. They speak of divine lessons. Songbirds, raptors, waterfowl, travel near when a loved one has passed. To comfort. But on this night, alone and unable to remember, the bird noise is a gloomy and menacing reminder of past betrayals of past trials and tribulations.

Thoughts travel back to the beginning, that initial tap on the shoulder. To wake each new day to exactly 5:55 a.m. displayed on the face of the bedside alarm clock. Insufficient days after returning to her home in the Pacific Northwest. That final round-trip flight between the Republic of South Africa and Oregon. Throughout the days, weeks and months, these three numbers found her. Together the five, five and five, appeared in addresses, on license plates, telephone numbers, invoices. The channel on the television set. Something was trying to get her attention. Dreams were filled with five doorways. Five clouds. Five rivers. Five trees. The big five.

Five is the number of Christ. The number for humanity. The number for hands, feet and head. The number of *love*. Love for God and man. *Is not love the key that opens hearts and doors to the soul's deepest desire?* she asks. *Are we not asked to love Creator with all our hearts, to love our neighbor as ourselves? How far must we stray from the same words, commandments mirrored in all of the world's holy books, before the weight sways?*

1999

A bright clear spring day in an otherwise drizzling Portland. She sees herself walking along a bustling Twenty-third Street. Twenty-third Street is an area filled with shops, restaurants, Mom and Pop creamery, ethnic and homestyle delicacies. Bookstores, high-end designer furniture showrooms, clothing and knick-knack emporiums. A cross between bohemian and upscale. Grunge and sophisticated.

In the windows of teahouses, bookstores and art galleries posters and fliers are taped, pinned, glued. A small handwritten note catches her eye. It reads, 'If something is trying to get your attention, call 503…'

Dialing the number. The man on the other end of the line speaks of being a 'double Virgo'. No nonsense, he states. "I am a man who holds a red pen." She furrows her brow with distaste for and of the red pen; with a quick stroke it kills creativity, flair and design. He says matter-of-factly that he is a tarot card reader by night. By day he serves as the mayor of a small town on the outskirts of Portland. Together they set a time for the coming Friday evening at six o'clock. This would be her first tarot reading. Was this black magic? Bad luck? Might it have negative consequences?

As a small child she was exposed to palmistry, astrology and numerology. Her older sister would illustrate in beautiful pictures, stunning colors, the twelve signs and placements of the houses, charted by the exact location of the planets at the moment and place of birth. A gift of an astrological birthday card for the upcoming year. Her moon in sensitive Pisces, a little fish in the deep blue ocean holding down all the planets above the mid-heaven as balloons held by strings.

Entering into the room in downtown Portland. The City of Roses, the City of Bridges. At exactly five minutes to six. Walls covered with the Major Arcana. Hand painted tarot cards span the height and width of the east-facing wall, enveloping her with a feeling of calm. She comes from a long line of artists. A playwright. A poet. A graphic designer, a sculptor and a musician. Laughter, libations and music filled the homes of her youth.

The sun card and the strength card sat side by side on the wall. The sun card, with a small child riding atop a white horse, sunflowers and sunlight gracing the background, a card for joy and happiness. The strength card, courage and beauty, pictures a fair maiden with garlands in her hair, leaning over to caress the king of the jungle. The card for Leo, her sun sign, the woman pictured is calm, however dominant over the lion.

Cards ranging from the lover's card to the Devil. The Queen of Coins, the Fool and the Magician. Intricately and painstakingly created. She takes a seat on the sofa to await her reading. In the center of their legs, sandwiched, there is a hardwood table. On the table is a magic eight ball — a toy for children. Shaken after a question is asked, the inky water reveals a small, multi-sided white plastic triangle, with one word or phrase to answer your question. 'Yes,' says the ball.

He explains how he works. "I will use the tarot cards to clarify what I receive working as a medium. I close my eyes and enter into what I call my 'workshop'. I will write down what words and phrases I am given."

His eyes closed, he begins to write on a clean piece of paper, slow at first, then more determined. He covers the entire length of each new page. Her eyes move from his face to the full moon outside the window, and finally come to rest back on the painted walls.

In time, he opens his eyes. He locks his on hers. "In the twenty-five years I've been doing this, I have never had the same word or phrase repeat itself more than two or three times, at most," he says. "You and I are going to argue. I ask you to hear me out first, and after you may dismiss me as a person, but do not dismiss what I have received from 'Other'. What I am about to reveal to you comes from 'Source'. My pages are filled with the word 'writer'. You will be a writer."

She says to herself, *He has mistaken me for my mother or for my sister.* They are the writers in the family. Remembering boarding school days where she had such terrible dyslexia, spelling was just another foreign language that required mastering.

He continues. "You will champion a cause, others would rather not. You will speak in front of hundreds, later thousands of people. People will give you money, vast sums of money, ensuring the success of this campaign." He continues. "I see you on television. I hear your voice on the radio. I read about you in national and international publications. You will win prestigious awards. I see you traveling — international and domestic. You will write a book. Your book will change the minds of celebrities, political leaders, heads of international conglomerates, friends and family." He carries on. "Inspired, they will pick up the mantle. They will create their own versions of this cause. Please," he stresses, "take note of these final words. There will be a time during this laser-focused mission where you will be asked to trust. If you choose fear, loss of faith, there will be dire consequences."

The Star card

The first card pulled by the clairvoyant was to show the importance of writing in her life. The World card was chosen. The World card: our hero has reached the goal, found the lost paradise. According to the law of the circle, everything that emanates from its center point is reflected back to it by the border of the circle. This makes the eclipse the symbol of a greater unity, uniting the original pairs of opposites like masculine and feminine, light and shadow, conscious and unconscious.

She wonders, knowingly. Does this mean that inside of her is the animus/anima, yin/yang, asleep/awake; is the world and all that there is in it, within her?

Within all people? Within all creatures, all things?

The next card flies out of his hand. Across the room. Lands face up. Chosen by pixies, sprites or spirits.

The Star card: fountain of youth, finally reaching the water of one's life; its secret is not the quality of the water, but the difficulty of finding it. After the walls have been blown up, and the dust has settled, the liberated soul sighs in relief and gathers new hope. She is aware, her past, present and future are intricately woven into the night sky.

Recollections of life while living in Johannesburg. The beauty of Africa and its people but, believing her life would end on that continent. Daily television stations broadcast violent crimes. Newspaper articles spanning page after page, murder, rape, kidnapping. Ex-pats as locals targeted. Framed against the bluest of skies, the deepest of canyons, 'God's Window'. The most glorious of mountain ranges, wildlife, animals, bushes and bloom. The kindest of people and one of the most exquisite harbors in the world, Cape Town.

The Wheel of Fortune after the question, 'How does one find their true purpose in life?' Seek the treasure that is hard to find, found by the four basic structures of the human consciousness. Thinking, feeling, sensing and intuition. This card represents luck, great fortune in all the tasks that we must accomplish in our lifetime.

The final card chosen is the Temperance Card: Temperance, the guide of the soul. The part that the card shows is a symbol of a narrow pathway to individuality, of becoming one's self, led (back) to the light.

Shivering

Involuntarily, as one does when one thinks of a rabbit hopping over one's grave. She longs for the sun to rise, for the light of day to return.

Speaking out loud, sharing her thoughts, emotions with the crow above. Be wise as the night owl perched statuesque on the far back, right side, of the vehicle. Protecting, watching over her. Believe in luck as the Wheel of Fortune card foretold.

"Trust, surrender. The tarot card reading. Trust and you will survive." She surrenders her thoughts, her emotions to the stars. Her international spiritual group asks each to offer up sincerely both heart and mind to God. Connect the inner unto the outer. Clean out all that has been handed down from parents and parents' parents. Hold onto what is of value. Allow the unwanted to be swept clean. Subud* recognized by the United Nations as a world organization fostering peace. Humanitarian bent. She knows in her heart of hearts that this connection holds panic at bay. The mind, fragile, a thin line between sanity and insanity.

She would find a love for writing so deep, so pleasing, equal to when she takes photographs. Taking comfort in viewing the letters that appear before her. The precise words that are in her heart. On her mind. She does not take credit for the letters, words, sentences, that shape stories. A collaborative effort. Trusting that it is along the etheric cord, an invisible pulley system, where imagination, creativity and spirit work in a perfect harmony that allows her to write. Conscious of when she was born, the breath of life given. The 'Raha'. A connection to last a lifetime.

The emergency lights

Flash hesitantly against the broken windows. She remembers the night her photographic coffee-table book, *African Journal: A Child's Continent*, was printed, bound, one copy handed to her. The remaining 3665 copies would be shrink-wrapped in packages of five, placed into boxes holding a total of thirty-five books each.

It was a winter evening in the Pacific Northwest, frost clung to the windows, she sat close to a soothing fire and read for the very first time her book, alone. As if another hand wrote. Tears. Unstoppable tears. Asking herself, *Who is this woman who traveled into unknown territory, placing herself into dangerous situations time and time again?* She knows that her question is rhetorical.

Its stories and images come to life as she lays cold in the white SUV. A story of survival and courage, a story to change an idea, an image. A story to change a belief. As a photographer, illuminated series of faces and recordings highlighting the forgotten orphans from Sub-Saharan Africa. Written, with the hope of a renewed sense of grace and dignity for the children, and for ourselves.

Inner-city, Johannesburg
Spring 2001

Inside the iron bars of the makeshift classroom, some children play, some children sleep. She has entered the city of Hillbrow. Once home to the wealthy, it now stands in ruins. She walks into a war zone. Poverty, crime and retribution choke the air. Broken windows hold clothing lines hung heavy with graying garments. Dark concrete walls are permanently scarred with tribal graffiti.

Up from tattered mattresses flattened by years of daily use, leap two sleeping sentries, teenaged outlooks, keeping guard over the babies inside. 'Power' introduces her to his attentive buddy, 'Freedom'. Eying her Nikon camera, he sizes it up in a moment for its street value. She hands over her new blue Nike knapsack, filled with lenses, filters and film. Guards dropped, prideful expressions, and unspoken trust in their stead. Her self-appointed bodyguards usher her into the classroom.

She first notices the absence of toys within the dank, dark and barren room. A room hoping to form minds, hearts and creativity for the next generation of consumers and workforce. A room hoping to form teachers, politicians, physicians and artists. It is impossible to take photographs of the children stampeding over one another in hopes of being the first to be picked up. The first to be noticed, each reaches out to be held. Power, freedom and she, after promises to return, heads to Toys 'R Us. Yes. Even in Africa.

They return hours later with crayons, puzzles, blocks, balls, all shapes and sizes, and a plastic telephone. The children are silent as each is given one gift. Mute. Nothing. Has she overdone it, playing the lady bountiful, embarrassing herself and the children?

The pied crow

Laughs his crow's laugh. Head tilting one way then the other. Remembering only yesterday when he flew high in the sky carrying a heavy tortoise; while resting on a branch, he let go of the turtle, dropping it to the ground below to break its shell. After, he ate its succulent, delicious, delicate white flesh.

 The laughter of the bird jolts her. She gathers up her morning travels like a childhood blanket. She had arrived early into Windhoek Airport, the capital of Namibia. Knowing that Namibia was a safe country. A country free from tribal disharmony. She rented a brand-new white Toyota 4x4 equipped with a cell phone and maps. Purchased two bottles of water, a bottle of Rescue Remedy, a homeopathic tincture for shock, stress or injury held in a tiny brown opaque glass bottle. She headed west towards the coast. The road ahead a straight uninterrupted line edging a carpet of tiny yellow flowers. Red boulders off in the distance. There was a sweetness coming off the desert floor and the sky was open. Out of the city lights, the blacktop disappears into loose sand and gravel.

Signposts were far and few, swept away by torrential rains. Liquid evaporates quickly, leaving behind parched orange and rust-colored earth. There was an absence of other vehicles. More donkeys, black-backed jackal and cattle than people and cars. In and out went the signal to the radio. She switched it off. Her eyes stick on the gas gauge. It is stuck in the 'full' position. With four hours' drive behind, and four to go before she was to reach the Desert Wilderness Lodge. Stop. Pull over, look at the map. A symbol for a gas station. She is at the center-point, halfway between the station and tonight's accommodation.

The truck's wheels bumped over cattle guards placed in the dirt to keep cattle in and prey out. Birds were singing, donkeys walked lazily down the side of the road, tails swishing at flies. She steered the truck hard, bumping down a washed-out dirt road, into a farm stall. There was a single gas-tank. An old-fashioned pump, the kind you must turn a crank to push the gasoline up and into the tank. An old man wearing a felt hat, sweat and toil staining a circle all the way around its crown, he had helped her. She watched as the setting sun, slow in its attempt to gobble up the nearly new moon in its entirety as it inhales the heat of the day; only to blow it out again at the crack of dawn.

She drove too fast around a sharp bend. The road dropped. There in front of her was an impala, its eyes frozen on the sparkle of the truck's brush-guard. She swerved out of control. The rear wheels skated sideways to the left, then lock right. Aiming for a three-foot embankment, she struggled with the steering wheel and lunged forward, hitting a tremendous boulder headfirst. The truck flipped. Crash test dummy, slow motion. An astronaut on the moon, legs and arms bounced. Her head concussed hard against the window. Far, far away along the straight line of the world, the sun had set.

A strong wind blows. The rain will follow shortly. *Is there anyone there?* She is sure she heard a sound. The cold is unbearable. A dream of a lion. He sits pressed up against the chassis of the truck. Patiently he waits for morning. God and the Devil are at war. There is a struggle deep within her body. Stripped, exposed, vulnerable. An animal on its nightly walk bumps the back of the truck; is it the lion? Has he come to lick the skin off her bones in two, three tries? Blade-sharp, thorny pinkish-black tongue.

Turning on the headlights. Seeing only the road ahead, in the distance, visible to the lights edge. In her left ear. Soft and seductive a voice says, *Sleep, all will be well.* While in her right ear, a voice angrily commands, *Wake! You must walk. You must find help.*

"One must never leave the vehicle," the Embassy representative had cautioned. But in Africa, all rules are broken. The temperature, unforgiving as it rises rapidly in Fahrenheit within the first hours of dawn. The desert with an absence of humidity, like a switch, on-off, fire and ice.

Count and pocket the three figs, the small bottle of Rescue Remedy and her passport. No water. Her camera gone. The passport is in case she does not make it back. Her family will at least be able to identify the body.

Remove all articles of clothing from the suitcase. Build a small nest where the window once was. She begs for a dream. Dream of all those that she loves. Asking to see their faces. Her daughter so like her in looks and equal. Her son so much her personality. Dream of her husband. His never-ending love for her. Anguish owns her heart; hopelessness fills the thoughts of her thinking.

The song "Let My Love Open the Door" by Van Morrison fills her head, soft and gentle. The music allows her to believe that the pressure on her head is her husband's hands that hold her together, that the blood might cease. That the separation may be erased. A song, he played over and over. When words failed him, music was the instrument of communication. Songs strung together as pearls, was his truest talent.

1999

The night of the tarot card reading, driving home. Her children away at university, her husband had remained in Johannesburg completing his projects. Her husband, nicknamed by coworkers the 'ambassador' for his extensive knowledge, understanding the verbiage of languages, the sales team and the mathematics, the designers, engineers in the international world of high-tech.

The night was cool and clean. The moon took up a large chunk of the sky, its wide smile, eyes lit up, laugh lines, called to her like an old friend. *Stay outside. Accompany me.*

She walked into their home, six miles from downtown Portland. Into the kitchen to pour a glass of vintage South African wine. Through the double Dutch, heavy walnut front doors of their cedar clad home to sit down on the front stoop nestled between two massive old Douglas fir trees. She looked up at the sky and yelled, "If you want something from me, then you had better shout!"

Bone tired, up the stairs to an empty bed. Climbing in, she reached over to turn off the bedside table light.

A vision. Standing beside her bed, a young African girl. Short black cropped hair, dark eyes. The little girl spoke her name as a gentle breeze. *Angel.* The color of her face changed as two thin lines turned her young brown skin translucent where tears fell from her eyes. With hushed Xhosa undertones, Angel shared that she carries the AIDS virus.

For the first time in months, she slept. Waking to a new day. Armed with the knowledge of her cause. Angel was asking her to return to Africa with her camera. A camera she has had in her hands since a teenager. To return to the country she loved. The country she feared. The country that could eat you up and spit you out whole. The country that held little value for human life.

It was as if a carpet had been laid out under each step taken. To sit next to a missionary on that first return flight back to Johannesburg, a man who would escort her into the refugee camps along the border of RSA and Mozambique. Other times, believing her reservation to board a bus bound for Soweto, as a tourist, only to be met in the hotel lobby by a slender young man holding a sign with her name on it. Together they would drive in his dilapidated, tiny automobile, into the center city of Johannesburg. She would explain why she had returned to the country that she loved and feared.

By the time they had reached the end of a long perfectly manicured hotel's driveway, under an umbrella of ancient jacaranda trees ablaze with purple blossoms, her new friend and driver would toss out his designated route. Rather, he would introduce her to a small orphanage inside the township of Soweto, one that he had called home.

Soweto
September 11th, 2001

It is early morning outside Johannesburg. She is in the squatters' camps. The day is dark, the temperature only slightly above freezing. The camp is a labyrinth of muddy crossroads. It is a maze of endless twists and turns, row upon row of metal sheeting, barbed wire fences, discarded cars, tires. Unprepared, she has worn flip-flops: it's hard to find dry footing in the rain and raw sewage.

The brown, wet streets frame the corrugated tin-walled and tin-roofed dwellings. Inside the structures, two rooms house up to twenty-four children, boys in one, girls in the other. Rain drips through the seam of the roofline. The children are barefoot. The only warmth comes from their faces, a steamy aura.

Huddled around a makeshift stove, they tell stories of watching mother and father die from an unknown sickness. Agonizingly long, slow and painful deaths are witnessed. Parents will be propped alongside the many others awaiting a proper burial.

The graveyards are full. Children are worried that their parents will never be buried.

To go to heaven, parents must be given the proper ritual: the purification wash and anointing, the nighttime vigil when the next of kin guard and bless the body. There is not one blood relative left to perform the ancient burial rite.

Unlike the children living in rural South Africa, the children of Soweto have some understanding of the AIDS virus, though their notions are part myth, part lie. The children have been told, the older children at least, that if they suspect they are infected, tell no one. An admission to the disease meant certain alienation, and possible murder. Later that same day she would learn of the devastation in the United States due to terrorist attacks, but it was she who was held and cared for by the orphans of Soweto.

Her family would be worried when she did not check in. Remembering her job, running the 'Q' Fund, a non-profit founded to aid vulnerable children from South East Asia to southern Africa. Chimoza Community School in Zambia, the NGO's flagship project was built, brick by brick, building after building, over a span of fifteen years.

A school offering small classrooms, for a better teacher-student ratio. Students chose the name and color for each newly erected school-block.

When children learned that there was a free school, they would take it upon themselves to rise early, fetch water, wash and dress, feed younger charges and walk the two hours each way in the dark to attend classes. Walking along the lips of busy roads with trucks stretched beyond capacity, overflowing, hauling copper south to the port of Durban, South Africa. Headed to China. Trucks that would fail, miserably, first-world countries' road safety tests.

Young pupils placed self-imposed restrictions of never being tardy, never being absent. A school where students' final test scores were some of the best, in the entire country.

The children she had met along the way knew intuitively there was nothing more sustainable, more essential than being given a solid education. Education is the single most important link out of an impoverished, societal mindset. Break the chains that muddle, that mimic, that mime. Allow students to realize dreams, talents, aspirations.

Looking back to interest groups, world organizations, NGOs, encountered throughout the years, some worked alongside. Far too many focused exclusively on helping girls, ignorant to the boys left behind. It is the boys who pick up guns.

She was appreciative; proficiencies had been handed down to her by her father. A highly decorated military man, ex-CIA. Her father had served back-to-back tours of duty from Normandy to Okinawa. General Westmorland in Vietnam demanded that her father flank him in battle. Her dad was her vanishing, varnished rock. A stone to carry in her pocket for bravery, for joy, for sorrow.

Summer
1997

Her husband's software company had sent him to South Africa for a two-year stint. Their small family of four had closed up their home in the Pacific Northwest, packed every unnecessary object into oversized trunks and said goodbye cheerfully to the rain and gray skies of the US west coast. They had previously transferred to England for a year on a similar billeting, but this African posting was their first truly exotic one. Unprepared. Innocence abroad. A quick read of Karen Blixen and Graham Greene — the only pertinent books on their shelves — did not, of course, introduce one to Africa, but to its colonial sins in beautiful prose.

In early fall she met her family in Johannesburg. Traveling there from Morocco. Completing an advanced course in the alternative medical field-mind/body discipline — part of an ongoing series of lectures she'd been attending for years.

She woke that first night in Marrakesh with some non-specific illness, most likely dysentery, that lasted days behind the walls of the Medina, in a palace in Morocco.

To lie on sateen sheets in a queen-sized bed with a high fever. Blood as thick as tar, unleashed, emptying out the contents of what was the width and breath of self.

Majestic, midnight black horses ridden by Arabian knights danced around the four walls, while monkeys shift-shaped from man to Hanuman, the magical Hindu monkey dressed in men's clothing, men's thoughts, men's deeds. Flies covered the plate of rice carried up the servants' staircase by Sophia: silently she came to the landing that met the bedroom door. "S'il vous plait, madam, a little rice is good."

Was it a dream or had she gone to the hammam and watched, huddled, from a corner in the ancient underground sauna? Arms wrapped tightly around legs pulled close into chest. Eyeing the round European ladies. Through a steamy curtain their naked bodies turned pink, as a pair of tiny hands scrubbed off dead skin with stiff, bristled brushes. And did she board the bus that went up the steep mountain road, rounding corners too close to its edge, to brave the Berber village? Sway with ghosts as they rose from the mossy green and moist brown earth, in the Atlas Mountains.

Still weak from the Morocco trip when her plane landed in Johannesburg, she was joined by her husband and children in a huge, rented house to the north. Stucco, yellow, pillared with French doors. English-style gardens, blue agapanthus, rose scented pelargoniums, bright orange and yellow gazanias plants. The smell of a freshly cut lawn. Digging for worms, miniature birds, bright red and green, locals nicknamed these tiny birds 'Christmas ornaments'. Polka dots against green grass, birds no bigger than a goldfinch surrounded the cool, turquoise water of a swimming pool. Winter was arriving in this hemisphere.

She hadn't expected the opulence, but was even less prepared for the squatters' camps rammed against the perimeter of the property. Security guards with automatic rifles patrolled the massive stone walls. She was not convinced that this was the ideal country to raise two teenagers.

A parent-teacher orientation was scheduled at her son's school for the following week to be held in the newly designed auditorium, on the grounds of the American International School of Johannesburg. Far north of the city center, nestled in the rolling hills of the horse country. Where the sky met the lavender fields.

She listened to an international medical relief organization's medic speak of the dire situation in Zambia. "In Zambia, the country's cry is 'Everyone is either infected or affected by AIDS'." It triggered in her mind the years spent in New York City as a high-fashion model in the seventies. HIV and AIDS were not yet diagnosed; however, something was making men sick. The fashion community was hit hard. Maybe Zambia was that second chance to not again sit back on the sidelines, but to pull up the boot straps, and do something.

Namibia had been the final country visited, collecting research. A reconnaissance mission peppered with photographs and articles. Incidents and accidents like parasites hitch-hiked her body during research. "Fail to plan, plan to fail." She heard her husband's favorite colloquialism. She had organized beforehand to meet with a missionary living along the border of Angola. A friend to the local Himba tribe would be her escort. Following their customs of introduction. Time and traditions in Africa are not the same as in countries whose citizens live by a timepiece, appointments, or self-imposed deadlines. Patience, a prerequisite Judgment, a mandatory mental softening.

Her silent promise: hold the reins loosely. *Do not leave an American footprint.* Sustainability was the key for any and all projects. The idea, 'teach a man to fish' was exemplary. However, one must first allow a traumatized child to recognize that he or she is loved, cared for. Play together as a mother to child, teacher with student, lay side by side on the dirt floor, color in coloring books, sing, dance. Long before instructions for learning alphabet, math, geometry on the 'talking walls' can commence.

She reflects now, today, taking a pregnant pause in her writing. In retrospect had she done more damage than good? Building a free community school educating thousands of vulnerable children. Pre-kindergarten to twelfth grade. Resigned to closing its doors when her husband was diagnosed with Lou Gehrig's disease. Would it have been better not to have built in the first place? An unanswered question as old as the ages.

The Southern Cross, visible in the night sky. A bowl of stars reaches from horizon to horizon, 180 degrees. The solar-system, upside-down. The Big and Small Dippers. The Jewelry Box, within the Milky Way, on fire with precious and semiprecious stones. She thinks back to her childhood; her mother and her father told bedtime stories, stargazing from sleeping bags near the massive cherry tree on the front lawn of their family home. "We come from the stars, and it is to the stars that we shall return." They would say, "We have stardust inside each of us." Her mother so loved her children, teaching each to care. The golden rule growing up in a family of eight was to be kind.

Sitting on the driver's side door of the vehicle, she can reach out to touch her star, the colors, shapes, many she had never seen before, so near, the one with her name wrapped around it. It seemed to shine brightest, comforting her; she felt that the star and she were one and the same. She looks to the second largest star. The star astronomers call the 'Lion Gateway'. One of three that light up the pyramids in Gaza, the Valley of the Kings and Queens. A spiritual light to open the way home.

Drifting off to sleep, hands tucked high up between her thighs for warmth. The spicy smell of gasoline burns her nostrils. All she can think of is water. Her mouth parched, she can barely swallow. Something large flies low over the crash as the cold air turns arctic around her. Maybe the owl, maybe a vulture. Birth. Death, new beginnings. Survivalist and resourceful. Paintings by the Dutch artist, Hieronymus Bosch, as words from the pages of

Dante's inferno fill the space as a cocoon. Vultures stand at the gates of Hell. "Do seraphs secure the seven realms of heaven?" she asks herself out loud.

Images appearing from the past. A book given years ago by a dear friend. Photographs of water, magnified, viewed. Research by a Japanese professor. Water collected from various places. A stream. A mountain runoff. Droplets of water studied under a microscope, showing the exquisite patterns of the water when classical music was played, when uplifting words were spoken. Or, if harsh expressions were shouted, distorted images, demonic shapes appeared on top of the thin glass slides.

What must the patterning of water look like in a newborn's heart? Lungs, brain, gut. An infant holds seventy-percent of itself in water in its body. Does the slide show ugliness, she muses, or do we glimpse a sliver of perfection?

Water that brings life to every organ in the body. She is curious to learn if exposed to fighting, to rage, must the body's fluid react in a hideous, negative fashion?

Planting seeds of retaliation, hatred, anger. Coding adverse 'isms', to fray the moral fiber. Setting up atypical cell structure. Young eyes that have seen only ugliness. Young ears that have heard only sadness. Is a new structure born?

She questions herself, *Aren't there pillars necessary to hold up love in human form?* Trust. Respect. Courage. Gratitude. Care. Kindness. Compassion. Joy. Words bring with them a childhood song, learning the bones of the human anatomy. The knee bone's connected to the thigh bone…The shoulder bone's connected to the arm bone…

Kindness is connected to care…Care is connected to being fully awake, alive. She hums to herself, distracting the boomerang of mozzies and flies bouncing between her ears and her eyes.

To be aware of another's state. 'Sleep knits the raveled sleeve of care' (Shakespeare).

Tap, tap, tap, the branches of a squat bush hit hard against the truck reminiscent of cymbals and a drum. The noise brings her back once again into the pages of *African Journal: A Child's Continent.*

Zimbabwe
2001

It's six o'clock in the morning. The day is cold, blustery, in Johannesburg; her breath is visible as she pulls tightly the outer layer of her clothing. Winter has arrived. She boards the S.A.A. flight bound for Victoria Falls. Emmanuel, her driver, will meet her tomorrow in the hotel lobby.

The Victoria Falls Hotel sits high above its namesake. The widest waterfall in the world stretches to bridge the distance between Zimbabwe and Zambia. Flamingo pink alabaster exterior walls frame black shutters, windows and doors. Tall, polished white columns hold long, low, patios that open up under the shade of the acacia trees. Entering into the foyer, trophies gaze down with frozen expressions as antique photographs of exotic birds, spotted leopards and white-faced monkeys stare back at her. Skins warm the ebony floor in shades of cream and chocolate.

The 'bush donkey' is the name locals have given to the zebra. Black and white stripes melt into one another along the grassy landscape that once was the breadbasket for Africa. Years of starvation, murder, death and disease leave a trail of bloodshed staining the ground where tall sweetcorn and lilies once grew.

A funeral procession passes by. She is told this happens throughout the days. It is said if a family member does not attend the funeral, they must be responsible for the death. He or she will be charged accordingly. The absent family member is the guilty party. Superstition forces people to leave jobs behind. A day or a week's loss of pay is guaranteed for those making the long journey back home. By foot, bus or taxi they travel to honor their dead. They are afraid if they do not arrive in time for the burial, additional family members will fall under an evil spell. Someone else will die.

Emmanuel takes her into his village. His village has a great number of AIDS affected orphans. They drive slowly along the side of a one-room schoolhouse. The creamy stucco building has a cobalt blue wooden door and window frames. On the playground there is a grid made up of rocks. Each different row indicates one grade level. Students choose the appropriate line before classes will begin. An old man sits on a chair and counts to see which new child is absent, presumably dead from the virus. The children wear uniforms without shoes, their dewy footprints visible on ice-crusted brown earth.

Her eyes catch the reflection in the interior mirror. It is her father's eyes that looked back at her. The palest hue of baby blue. A color so rare only a hummingbird can truly appreciate this shade. Her father dead for many years. The lips that appear on her face are those of her grandmother, ruby red lipstick. Her grandmother, a tall Irish beauty, born in a time when manners maketh the man.

Blood cakes her forehead, cheeks and chin. She does not see herself reflected back. Try as she might to pull up a memory of her Gamma.

Age six: she and her two older sisters would wear Gamma's originally designed 'poodle skirts' paired with hand-knitted sweaters, embroidered in pearls on felt cut-outs of dogs, cats and/or birds. She was a living doll for her sisters; one entire can of hairspray made her waist-long blond hair stiff, high heels as accoutrements and, the pièce de résistance, her grandmother's matching pocketbook. The clickety-click of a Kodak instamatic camera in sync with each step on hardwood floors in four-inch heels. Make-up and runway. Their three brothers would look up from building model airplanes, roll their eyes and giggle.

Hoisting

Herself up through the driver's side door of the vehicle, she sits outside once again. This time she opens her heart to the deities of mythology. *Goddesses who created the world*, she begs, *please pour bravery into my vessel*. She listens to the sounds of the desert. She believes she hears low conversations between the dwarf shrub bushes and the sand. Sand swells up as a baby cobra, as if to articulate off the tip of its ineffective forked tongue. *If you walk, we will meet the soles of your feet so that nothing stirs. Predators will be unaware of your presence.* Her ribs ache, her teeth rattle. She cannot find her glasses. The blow to her head has made the simplest reasoning impossible: which is the greater number? Which is the greater distance? The thirteen kilometers back to the farm, or the thirty-six kilometers to the village ahead. Solitude? A village named Solitude. Is thirteen greater the thirty-six? So many threes.

It is the night's darkest point. The sun will rise shortly. Bury her urine in the sand. During the night, three sets of prints have circled the truck: a donkey's, the impala, and the third, a cat. A small one, but that's no comfort. What creatures had heard, sensed, smelled her throughout the long night and days.

She sends a kiss, gratitude to the stars, the sun and the moon that kept watch over her. Giving her resolve, the courage to exit the truck. She does not know why she was not attacked. She does not know why she was not killed. A drowning mix of body fluid and gasoline poisoned the air. *Walk in the direction opposite the village called Solitude.* Loneliness was the coat she had unintentionally grabbed on her way out the door so many years before.

The three figs. A small bottle of remedy. Tie the handkerchief around her head. An insignificant shield from the coming sun. Each breath, a spasm, her chest, one, two or three ribs broken where the seatbelt caught, clutched and held her. The bleeding from her head has finally ceased.

The sand reaches up to tickle the bottom of her feet; the air all around her parts as icebreakers that slowly make their way forward in the waters of the Arctic do for large ships. The bushes chuckle as if to say, *Do not interrupt the particles that make up this atmosphere*. Animals have keen instincts.

Walk, glide as taught a lifetime ago at the Rudolf Steiner School. A eurythmic. Do not break the flow of this arid terrain. Heel, toe. Heel, toe. She leans over to put on her hiking boots. Vertigo. Tie up the laces. Drained. Dehydrated. The pounding inside of her head is that final crescendo, percussions. Beethoven's Fifth Symphony.

She walks a short distance. Suddenly, a movement, a noise in front of her. Hard to discern between the crow squawking frantically in announcement. Crow so close she wonders if he were inclined to make a nest out of her disheveled hair. Was it a man or animal walking out of the rising sun, moving towards her deliberately, unhurried? Bellowing pale gray haloed against the blinding light of a new day. It is a baboon. Large. Old. Gray coat. Yellow teeth. Why is it alone, like her? Has it come to hurt her?

The primate sits up on a boulder. Sometimes to her left. Other times behind her. Picking at its hair. Grooming itself. Never looking at her face, never into her eyes. Not threatening. She hears the noise the birds make when a leopard is nearby. Where is the baboon's family? She wonders if he has come to offer himself up, if predator comes to drag her away. She loves him and calls him her friend and fellow traveler.

Sit, rest on top of the sand. Her passport falls from her pocket. Looking at the different countries' stamps, announcing each entry and exit. The towns, villages and cities. Remote areas where no one had seen a white woman. Her lips so dry, she cannot lick them, her tongue sticks into the cracks, the splits. A jackass passes. No people. Should she drink her urine? Removing one of her hiking boots to use as a cup. She pees. It is the color of dirty river water, dark smoky brown. Is she bleeding internally? She has not had food nor water in days.

She must lie down, curl up on the still, cool, dry ground. She remembers in Mozambique taking a stick to draw pictures in the sand, homes, animals and people, as she and the children did not speak one another's native tongue. Reaching out to pick up a stone to write a note in the sand for her children. *Please forgive me*.

Are there scorpions near, snakes? The Namaqua adder, terracotta in color, it lays in wait camouflaged just under the orange sand. Should she try to catch the passing donkey, ride it out of the desert. She laughs. The noise that comes from her. Unrecognizable. Her body is heavy as she melts into the vortex of a mother's earthly embrace. Sleep overtakes.

Dreamscape…

She walks through tall wheat colored grass; the tips sway back and forth in a gentle breeze; tiny little circles hold the pods where the seeds are stored. She follows a man. He wears a white cloak; in his right hand he carries a cane. The sky is clear, and the temperature is mild. The grass opens up. Children sit on matted down grass at play. Happy songs and laughter are heard. The man she follows now is a Zulu warrior; he wears the patchwork skin of the impala thrown over his right shoulder. Tied around his waist is the spotted pattern of the leopard. His throat is adorned with the teeth of a lion strung from its gut. Feathers, bits of tin and beads adorn his ankles and wrists. There is a constant, dull chime, sounds of his passing. Barefoot he carries his shield and a spear. The children playing stand up and follow. The older ones take the hands of the younger ones and carry the babies on their hips. The children wear torn clothing; some dress in school uniforms. Others wear nothing at all, and most are barefoot. The man she follows is now a woman. The woman she follows turns to face her. She looks into her eyes; they are her eyes.

She is the woman that she follows. She is the man that she follows. She is the children that she follows.

A commotion of birds fighting, pecking at her, bloodcurdling cries, wake her.

Why? Why did I have to wake?

Her dreams were occupied, fragrant, musty, miraculous and real. Family, friends, laugher. The favorite places of her youth. Swimming in a clear, clean, cool, lake in summer, horseback riding through meadows at a full gallop. Laying in a field of wildflowers where rabbits and field mice play. Mountains. Snow. Wind. Joy. Youth.

Get up and walk, she speaks out loud. *Walk.* It is so hot, too hot. Daydreams are filled with images of children's faces, their smiles, students from Ski Lanka to Africa.

She recalls little Moses, one of the first students attending her Chimoza School in Zambia; a child from the streets, the city center, he would come running up the long, rutted drive. The dirt road narrowing beyond the dilapidated blue and white police station. A police station without windows, doors or bars. Its only occupants, men who had enjoyed too much 'shake shake', a local brew made from maize and cassava. A starchy tuberous root. The staple diet.

The Chimoza School, an oasis on the grounds of an abandoned copper mine. One could reach up and pluck mangos, papayas, avocados, oranges, lemons and limes from its lush orchards. Moses would take her hand and not let go. When she prepared to leave, to return home to the United States, he would call her, taking hold of her arm, running his fingers up and down the soft blond hair of her forearm. "This, flies high in the sky in the big airplane, but, Momma," placing his little hand on top of her heart, "this will never leave me."

The baboon is too close; is it he and the crow that fight? Fear washes over her as a wave from a distant shore. Is this what the orphaned children feel? She remembers their ready smiles when all around them is poverty, the destitute, their sickness. How children only cried when a loved one has passed. Or if they themselves were gravely ill. That the smallest gift was received with gratitude and glee. Thinking back. The years essential to build trust. Trust, to unlock truth. The courage to speak of one's past, when secrets are held, locked inside young hearts; a lifetime of unnatural silence.

She sees their faces, their smiles. Tens of thousands of African children line both sides of the dirt road. She hears them calling to her. *Momma, please, one more step.* She sees her own children. How lucky to have two healthy, happy and caring adult children. The two halves of her heart.

She sees her husband: his favorite song plays in her head. Van Morrison's *Have I told you lately that I love you?* Songs were his language of love. One song out of three hours playing time, a compilation, continuous music. He would sit days on end with earphones on, orchestrating his memorial service. His own last rites. Songs to be played at his service, as one would choose their wedding tunes. She did not know then that each melody was chosen as a love song to her, his wife.

Baboon and crow are never far. Crow is not alone; his family join, creating a dark ring overhead. Black-backed jackal comes close. Crow family scream their exit. No families riding atop wagons. Nothing. Just a dirt road.

The haze cast by the sun creates shadows, hallucinations. Rolling up her shirt, bruises begin to form, roadmaps on a broken body.

A red feather
March 23rd, 2016

It was the final days prior to his death. Her husband, lover, friend for thirty-three years. Six-foot-eight, funny, handsome, away more often than not. Friends said he led the room with a smile and listened to what people had to say. He was a good man.

The words spoken to their family, a family he loved dearly, his perfect triangle. When the news of a diagnosis of A.L.S. arrived on his birthday he voiced, "When I can no longer speak the words on my mind, nor stand on my own two feet, I will be leaving you."

They had grown close, closer, becoming as one. She, his hands, his arms. They laughed. They cried. At times remained in bed for days on end, reminiscing the ups and downs of their lives together. The double helix strand. When he was down, she was up. When she was down, he was up; there was no greater love, intimacy, joy, passion than at the helix intersection.

He would call out to her. "Come, rest on top of me." Like a starfish she would lie with her arms, legs mirroring his. Being shorter, her head would land perfectly over his heart. He would breathe in, saying, "You are my energy, my fill-up station; your energy is goodness and love."

Three days before her husband died their family clung together. He fell from their California king-sized bed three times. He hated bothering people, sad and embarrassed to inconvenience the fireman. They adored him. It took all four first responders to lift him back up and onto their bed. Dead weight. He had lost the use of his arms and beautiful hands so long ago.

The last days their children spent days and nights speaking to their father, reminiscing all the worldly and wonderful places they had visited, they had lived, the special times shared. Calm and resolution filled their bedroom.

She placed his earphones on his ears and turned up the volume. She washed his face, hands and feet with essential oils. Lavender, frankincense and myrrh. He had grown a luxurious beard. To her, he looked like a holy man. His soft, youthful tanned skin, slender body, a dry sense of humor under ever-playful eyes. She pulled on a clean pair of winter socks over his feet. He did not like the cold.

The angels and archangels began to arrive. The first to emerge was so small, 'to an enormous angel, so tall it had to bend over to fit inside the four walls, under the ten-foot ceiling, a wingspan to engulf their entire bedroom.

Coming from the Bose headset she heard the song play, Warren Zevon's *Keep me in your Heart*.

Mourning doves

Climbing into bed beside him, listening to his breath slow. Talking to him, she tells him, "It's all right to leave us." Before he lost his voice, he spoke of seeing both his parents, many years gone. Old friends, his family, some who had passed, others living.

She does not want to leave him, but for a moment to tell their son and daughter, their father has passed. Walking from their bedroom she spooks a pair of mourning doves nesting inside the single pot of hanging geraniums, hanging from the side veranda which overlooks a canal from their newly built home in Charleston, South Carolina. Once outside she picks a handful of new rosebuds, pinks, reds and whites, shaking off the fresh thin layer of frost, making a small bouquet for his hands. She calls the funeral home then returns back under the covers, close, as close as possible.

Thoughts return. The time he had asked her, *Where do you think the soul goes after the body dies?* Her answer came as another question. *Maybe to the place that's in 'your' mind? The place 'you' believe it does.*

Her older brother had expressed these words to her many years ago. A few short months before his passing. An artist. Friends in the artist community spoke of him as becoming the next Wassily Kandinsky. Her brother would spend days working out mathematical equations prior to picking up a sketch pad, pencil, paint brush or pastels.

Walking from their bedroom. A song came to her. A melody she'd not heard in years. The Seekers, *I'll Never Find Another You.*

Wherever she went, feathers would fall from the sky, landing on her head, her shoulders, at her feet. Blue ones, red, white, black or, brown. Long ones, short ones. Hawks, eagles, bluebirds, woodpeckers. She had shared with her husband, during his final days, saying, *The cardinals are the highest of the songbirds*. She knew that her husband had listened when she spoke of the birds being the connection between heaven and earth. A red feather was left at the entrance of their home three days after his passing. It was Easter morning.

She gives thanks

To the crow and the old baboon for guarding her, accompanying her. For being her companions. Her friends. There were times when the baboon was far off in front of her, as if to say, *Come-on, it's safe*. Hyena's chalk white spore told a very different story.

Her walk moves slowly and steadily forward. Friends call her turtle. Turtle in Native American lore symbolizes healing, steadfastness and protection. 'It's turtles all the way down.' In South East Asia, there is a belief that the entire world was created by sand carried up from the deep sea on the backs of turtles.

She wishes she could have done more for the baboon; she realizes that when he turns his back on her. He will walk away to become one with the red African landscape, dust to dust. Buzzards and hyena will clean his carcass, releasing his spirit to travel unencumbered to where baboons go.

She does not remember much of the long walk. The headache, blinding, deafening, throbbing, heavy. The sun scorching.

Against all odds

A hunter inoculating sheep in his field spots her. The cattle guards just coming into view. He walks hastily towards her, leans over, with strong arms, to scoop her up off the sand. Tears come. The hunter holds her as if a child, she clinging to him as a child. He carries her into the farmhouse. His wife places her, fully clothed into a warm bath, knowing when severe dehydration sets, one must recapture water through the pores to offset a heart attack. The hunter asking how had she walked out of the desert? Was she alone? Where had she come from? Too many questions.

The tow truck came, with chains, flipping the truck. Her camera crushed. The water bottles crumpled. Her knapsack, ripped open, old photographs lay flat as cold case files, retrieved from the bottom of the stack. Slashed images look up at her, the faces of African children, other photos she had captured of lions, leopards, rhinos, cheetahs so close to smell their strong, stale, hot breath.

Thirty-two hours later in the Windhoek hospital, the man that lay in the bed next to hers is surrounded by his entire family. He had been bitten by a snake in his home. In his bed. It was the night a family's heart would break.

Outside her hospital window, creating a pattern, hundreds of crows fill the branches of tall mopane trees, new green leaves just beginning to peek out as they emerge and unfold. And from the crows fall feathers, shimmering black feathers. She knows that she was never alone. The souls of departed loved ones stand around her bed as the sentinels of Sossusvlei.

Say not, 'I have found the truth', but rather, 'I have found a truth'.

Say not, 'I have found the path of the soul'. Say rather, 'I have met the soul walking upon my path'.

Kahlil Gibran